Penguins

Original text by Luther Reimer

What are penguins?

Penguins are birds, but they can't fly.

Where penguins live

Penguins live by the sea in the southern part of the world. There are penguins on the coasts of South America, South Africa, Australia and New Zealand. There are also lots of penguins in Antarctica. There are no penguins in North America, Europe or Asia.

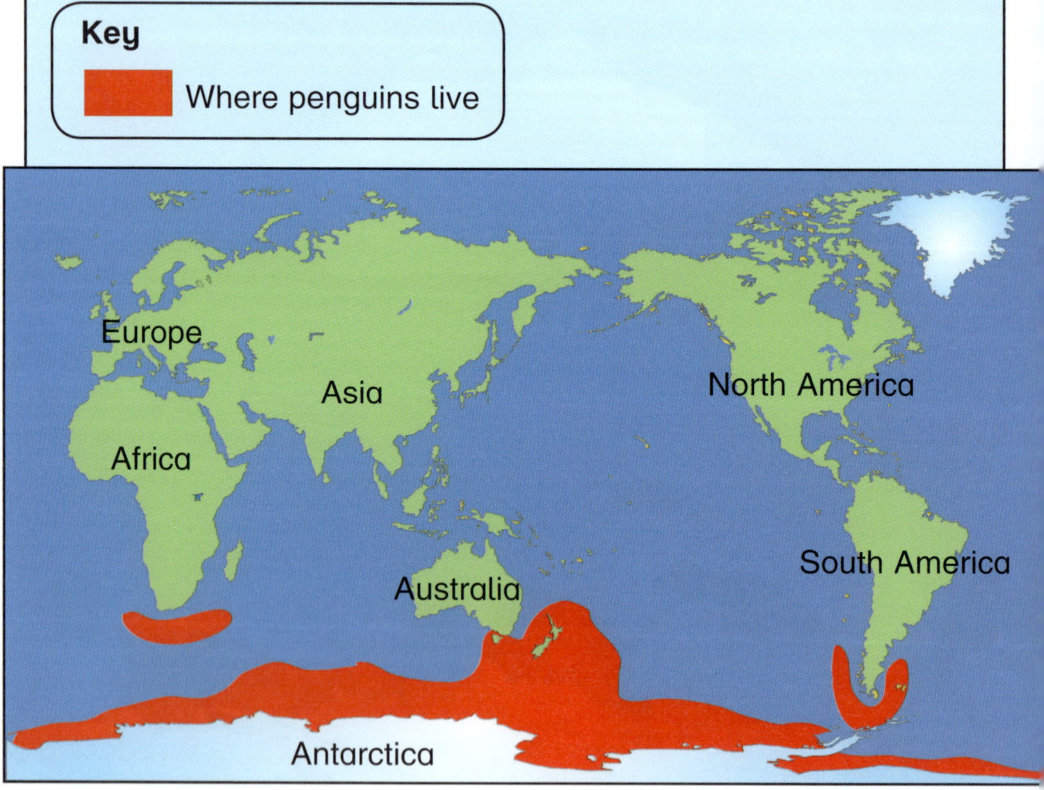

Different types of penguins

There are 17 different types of penguins. Emperor Penguins are bigger than all other penguins. They are 1.2 metres tall and they weigh 30-40 kilograms. In winter Emperor Penguins live on the ice around the Antarctic continent. It is very cold. It can be -60°C.

Height of an Emperor Penguin

Emperor Penguins don't make nests. The male penguin keeps the egg warm on his feet. The female penguin goes to the sea and eats. After 9 weeks she comes back and gives the baby food. The male penguin is very hungry! He goes to find food. In the summer all the penguins go to the sea again.

A male Emperor Penguin with an egg on his feet

Little Blue Penguins are smaller than other penguins. They are 41-44 centimetres tall and they weigh 0.9 kilograms. They live on the south coast of Australia, in Tasmania and on lots of islands near New Zealand. In the daytime they swim in the sea and at night they sleep in nests on the beach.

A Little Blue Penguin

Most penguins are black and white. Rockhopper Penguins have got yellow feathers above their eyes. They have got red eyes and an orange bill. Rockhopper Penguins are very aggressive and noisy. Sometimes they attack each other.

A Rockhopper Penguin

Rockhopper Penguins have this name because they can hop and jump very well. They can climb too. They make nests on high rocks.

Rockhopper Penguins can hop very well.

What penguins eat

Penguins eat a lot of food. All their food is from the sea. They eat fish, squid and krill. Krill are like shrimp. Penguins do not chew their food. They eat their food whole.

Penguin food

Penguins can dive very well. They dive into the sea to find food. Emperor Penguins are excellent divers. They dive very deep to catch the bigger fish. They can dive 300 metres and they can stay under the water for 20 minutes.

Penguins dive for food.

How penguins swim

Penguins have got two wings. Their wings are like flippers, so they can't fly. They use their wings to swim under the water. The feathers on their body and wings are waterproof. Penguins have webbed feet like ducks. They use their feet to change direction.

Parts of a penguin

1	webbed feet	2	waterproof feathers
3	short legs	4	bill
5	wings like flippers	6	head
7	eye	8	thick skin

Emperor Penguins can swim 10-15 kilometres per hour. They swim fast to escape Leopard Seals. Leopard Seals eat penguins.

A Leopard Seal

When penguins are close to land, they swim near the top of the water. Then they jump out of the water onto the land. Penguins can jump high.

Penguins jump out of the water onto land.

Penguins on land

Penguins have got short legs. They waddle when they walk. They use their wings to help them balance.

Penguins waddle on the ice.

Sometimes penguins move on their stomachs. They use their wings and feet to move on the ice and snow.

Penguins move on their stomachs.

When it is very cold, penguins huddle in groups. Then they feel warm. The penguins in the centre are warmer than the other penguins, so they change position.

Penguins huddle to stay warm.

The race to the South Pole

Written by Cheryl Palin
Illustrated by Stephen May

Captain Robert Falcon Scott wanted to be the first man at the South Pole. In 1901, he travelled to Antarctica, but the weather was very bad. He didn't see the South Pole. He was very disappointed.

In 1910, Captain Scott sailed to Antarctica again. He sailed from New Zealand in his ship, *Terra Nova.*

Six months later, *Terra Nova* arrived in McMurdo Sound, Antarctica. It was January 1911.

It was winter in Antarctica. Scott and his team didn't travel to the South Pole immediately. They lived in a hut on Ross Island. They prepared the expedition and they did scientific experiments.

In the summer the men started their journey to the South Pole. Captain Scott was very determined.
I'm going to be the first man at the South Pole!
But then they received a message.
TELEGRAM
Dear Captain Scott
I wanted to go to the North Pole, but an American called Robert Peary arrived there first. Now I'm going to the South Pole.
Good Luck!
Roald Amundsen
Oh no!
I don't believe it!
TELEGRAM

Roald Amundsen was an explorer from Norway. He wanted to be the first man at the South Pole. He sailed to Antarctica in his ship, *Fram*. Amundsen arrived at Ross Island in January 1911 too. His team camped on the other side of the island.

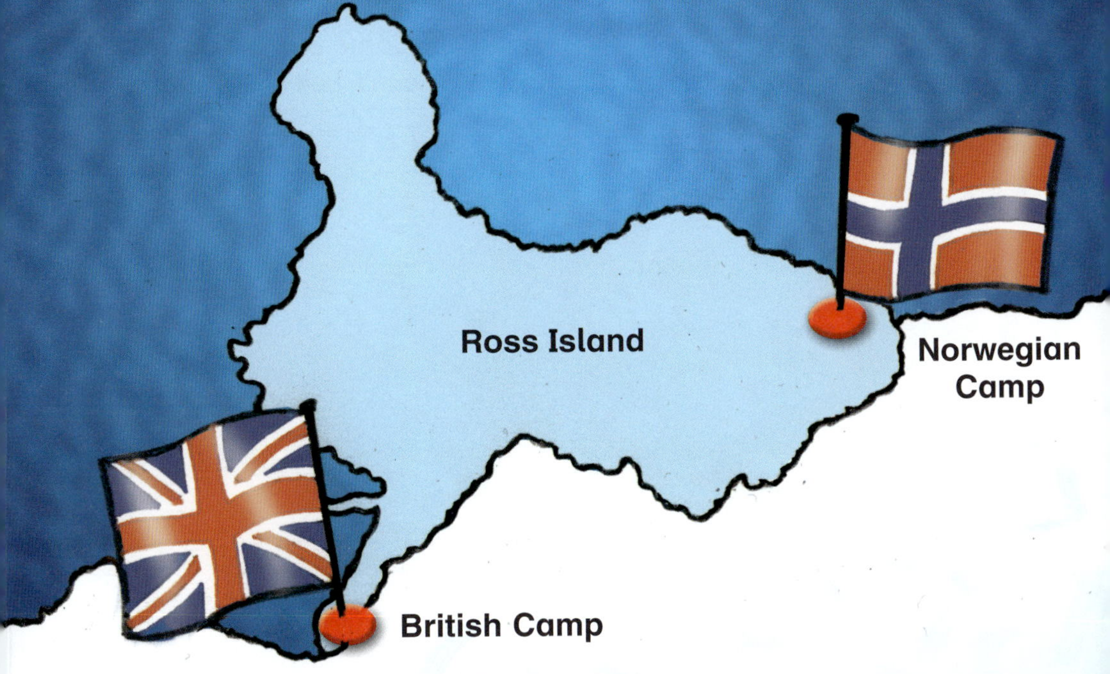

The journey for Captain Scott and his men was very difficult. There was lots of snow and ice. Scott's ponies were from Siberia. They were not very big and the snow was deep. Scott and his men pulled the sledges.

The food in the British camp was horrible. There was no fresh food. The men were not very strong. They were very hungry and cold.

The journey for the Norwegians was difficult too. But Amundsen's dogs were stronger than the Siberian ponies. They pulled the heavy sledges 100 kilometres every day. They pulled the men on skis too.

There was more food in Amundsen's camp. The Norwegians were warmer than the British. Their clothes were made of fur and animal skin. They looked like the Inuit people of Greenland.

In November 1911, Amundsen and his men were near the South Pole. They walked and walked in the snow. They climbed a dangerous glacier with ropes.

Then there was a terrible storm. They stayed in the tent for two weeks.

When the storm finished they continued their journey. On Friday 14th December 1911, they arrived. They were the first men at the South Pole.

Amundsen and his team put up the Norwegian flag. They stayed at the South Pole for three days. They skied around the pole. Then they travelled home.

When Amundsen arrived at the South Pole, Captain Scott and his men were still 640 kilometres away. On New Year's Day 1912, they arrived at the polar plateau.
We're nearly there.
Great!
We're the first!
The men were very proud and excited. But then ...
What's that? Is it a camp?
Yes! I can see a flag.
Look! Footprints!
Amundsen!

Two days later, on 17th January 1912, Scott and his team arrived. But they were not the first team at the South Pole. The Norwegians were the first. The brave explorers were very disappointed.
This is a horrible place.
s. Why did we come here?
I don't know. Let's go home.

Captain Scott and his brave team walked for many kilometres in very bad weather conditions. Finally two of the men, Evans and Oates, died. There were only three members of the team left. There was a terrible storm and they stayed in their tent. The men were very hungry and weak.

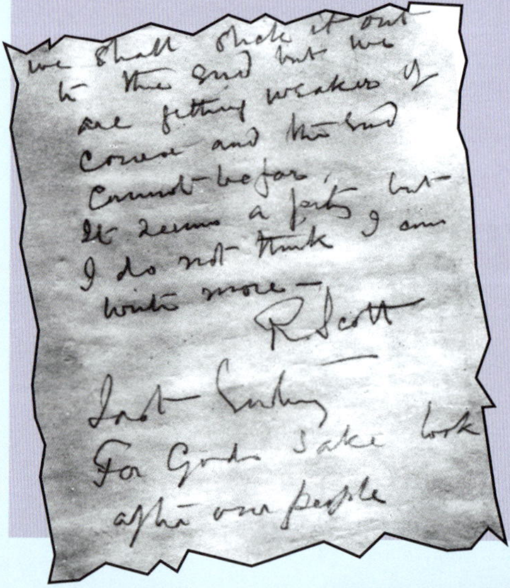

We shall stick it out to the end but we are getting weaker of course and the end cannot be far, It seems a pity but I do not think I can write more – R Scott

Last entry For God's sake look after our people

Scott, Wilson and Bowers didn't survive the expedition. In the summer a search party looked for Scott's camp. The tent was under lots of snow. Scott's diary and his letters were in the tent. This is how we know the story of Scott's terrible journey to the South Pole.

Activities

1 Find and match the words.

p	e	n	g	u	i	n	a	r	e
a	g	o	p	r	a	e	s	o	t
b	g	a	e	s	n	s	b	c	u
i	m	o	r	o	d	t	l	k	c
l	b	s	t	f	o	r	k	c	k
l	f	e	a	t	h	e	r	s	a
u	i	a	y	e	i	a	r	o	w
k	p	l	l	w	s	q	u	i	d

2 Write *E* for Emperor Penguins, *L* for Little Blue Penguins and *R* for Rockhopper Penguins.

1 They can't fly. E, L, R

2 They are 1.2 metres tall. ______

3 They have got yellow feathers above their eyes. ______

4 They eat fish. ______

5 They are very noisy. ______

6 They are black and white. ______

7 They make nests. ______

8 They weigh 0.9 kilograms. ______

9 They have got red eyes. ______

10 They live by the sea. ______

3 Complete the sentences.

1 Rockhopper Penguins are small. Little Blue Penguins are smaller.

2 Little Blue Penguins dive deep. Emperor Penguins dive ________.

3 Leopard Seals swim fast. Emperor Penguins swim ________.

4 King Penguins are big. Emperor Penguins are ________.

5 Little Blue Penguins hop high. Rockhopper Penguins hop ______.

6 In summer Antarctica is cold. In winter it's ________________.

4 Look at the notes and write about the Gentoo penguins.

Gentoo Penguins live in Antarctica on ________________

____

____

____.

5 Number the sentences in the correct order.

☐ Captain Scott and his team arrived at the South Pole.

☐ The British men started the journey to the South Pole.

☐ The British men saw the Norwegian flag.

1 *Terra Nova* sailed from New Zealand.

☐ The British men camped on Ross Island.

☐ Amundsen and his team arrived at the South Pole.

☐ A search party looked for Scott's tent.

6 Look and write.

7 Answer the questions.

1 Was Captain Scott British? Yes, he was.

2 Was Amundsen American? ________

3 Was it very cold in Antarctica? ________

4 Was the food in the British camp delicious? ________

5 Was the journey to the South Pole easy? ________

6 Was Amundsen the first man at the South Pole? ________

7 Was Scott the first man at the South Pole? ________

8 Was Scott disappointed? ________

8 Complete the story with words in the box.

disappointed ~~first~~ South Pole
sailed lived message
was six summer
wanted sledges December

Captain Scott wanted to be the (1) first man at the (2) ________. His ship *Terra Nova* (3) ________ from New Zealand in 1910. They arrived (4) ________ months later. Scott and his team (5) ________ in a hut on Ross Island. In the (6) ________ they started the journey to the South Pole. But they received a (7) ________. Amundsen (8) ________ to be the first man at the South Pole too. Scott's journey (9) ________ very difficult. The (10) ________ were very heavy. On 14th (11) ________ 1911, Amundsen arrived at the South Pole. Scott arrived 33 days later. He was very (12) ________.

Bilingual Dictionary

Write the words in your language.

beach	______________	noisy	______________
bill	______________	Norwegian	______________
brave	______________	penguin	______________
British	______________	ponies	______________
camp	______________	rock	______________
determined	______________	rope	______________
diary	______________	sail	______________
disappointed	______________	scary	______________
dive	______________	seal	______________
feather	______________	skis	______________
flag	______________	sledge	______________
footprint	______________	South Pole	______________
freezing	______________	squid	______________
fur	______________	stomach	______________
glacier	______________	tent	______________
high	______________	warm	______________
hop	______________	weigh	______________
hut	______________	wings	______________
ice	______________		
island	______________		
journey	______________		
message	______________		
nest	______________		

Macmillan Education
4 Crinan Street
London N1 9XW
A division of Springer Nature Limited
Companies and representatives throughout the world

ISBN 978-1-3800-3779-4
ISBN 978-1-3800-3778-7 (International Edition)

First published 2005
This edition published 2019

Illustrated by Stephen May

The authors and publishers would like to thank the following for permission to reproduce their photographs:

Cover image by Digital Stock

AKG Images p26(b) ©British Library, London; Alamy Stock Photo/mauritius images GmbH p9, Alamy Stock Photo/Nature Picture Library p14, Alamy Stock Photo/Yuen Man Cheung p5; Bryan and Cherry Alexander Photography p4; Corbis 26(t) ©Bettmann; Corbis/Royalty Free p12; Creatas p6; Getty Images/Corbis/Fuse p7, Getty Images/iStock/Musat p10, Getty Images/iStock/S_Lew p11(b); NHPA p11(t); Springer Nature Limited/Macmillan Australia p2; Stock Image Group/Minden/FLPA p13

Royalty free pp2, 7

Printed and bound in Great Britain by Bell and Bain Ltd, Glasgow

2023 2022 2021 2020 2019
10 9 8 7 6 5 4 3 2 1